THIS BOOK BELONGS TO...

Name:		Age:

Favourite player:

2022/2023

My Predictions...	Actual...
The Saints' final position:	
The Saints' top scorer:	
Premier League winners:	
Premier League top scorer:	
FA Cup winners:	
EFL Cup winners:	

Contributors: Peter Rogers

A TWOCAN PUBLICATION

©2022. Published by twocan under licence from Southampton Football Club.

Every effort has been made to ensure the accuracy of information within this publication but the publishers cannot be held responsible for any errors or omissions. Views expressed are those of the authors and do not necessarily represent those of the publishers or the football club. All rights reserved.

ISBN: 978-1-914588-74-7

£9

3

CONTENTS

GOAL
OF THE
SEASON

JAMES
WARD-PROWSE
PREMIER LEAGUE V WOLVES

The 2021/22 season saw Southampton strike 63 times in all competitions, among which there were some very strong contenders for the sought-after Goal of the Season accolade.

The name James Ward-Prowse is already synonymous with mouth-watering free-kicks, but the midfielder unleashed perhaps his greatest ever during Southampton's visit to Wolves at Molineux in January, beating José Sá in superb fashion as Saints looked to steal a point on the road.

Both teams arrived in good form, Southampton buoyed after a comfortable 4-1 victory over Brentford, and Wolves after a 3-0 win against Sheffield United.

Despite a strong start, Ralph Hasenhüttl's men found themselves behind to Raul Jimenez's penalty five minutes before half-time, a lead which was doubled moments before the hour mark after Conor Coady nodded home to put Bruno Lage's side in the driving seat.

However, with Saints in desperate need of a goal, nerves were instilled into the home crowd on 84 minutes, as set-piece specialist Ward-Prowse stood over a 35-yard free-kick.

Considering the Englishman's trademark side-footed, whipped approach to ensure the ball gets up and over the wall, many assessed that the opportunity may be a little too far out even for a man of Ward-Prowse's quality. How wrong they were.

Opting to drive through the ball with his laces, the strike was pure, arching slightly left before swerving violently right in-flight to bamboozle Wolves keeper Sa and nestle into his top-left corner. An exceptional strike and one which ultimately didn't deserve to be on the losing side that day.

STUART
ARMSTRONG
FA CUP V COVENTRY

ROMAIN
PERRAUD

FA CUP V WEST HAM

Southampton marched into the FA Cup fifth round following a hard-fought 2-1 win over Coventry, during which the home fans at St Mary's were treated to a Stuart Armstrong beauty.

The Scot, slightly right of centre, cutting across the ball with his right foot from 25 yards, arching his effort beautifully into the far corner.

Continuing their fine FA Cup form, Southampton progressed into the quarter-finals following a superb 3-1 victory over West Ham in which the scoring was opened courtesy of a Romain Perraud rocket.

The Frenchman powering his left-footed effort from distance across goal and into Alphonse Areola's left corner, the aggressive movement on the ball leaving his fellow countryman with no chance.

NUMBER OF SEASONS WITH THE SAINTS:

5

SOUTHAMPTON APPEARANCES:

242

SOUTHAMPTON GOALS:

0

PLAYER OF THE SEASON:

1984/85
1985/86

LEGEND

PETER SHILTON

SOUTHAMPTON ACHIEVEMENTS:

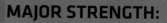

Four PFA First Division Team of the Season inclusions (1982/83, 1983/84, 1984/85, 1985/86).

MAJOR STRENGTH:

Springing from post to post with immense flexibility.

INTERNATIONAL ACTION:

No one in the history of the England men's national team has played for the Three Lions more than Shilton's 125. The legendary shot-stopper was a semi-finalist at Italia 90, but was beaten by Diego Maradona's infamous 'Hand of God' goal at the previous World Cup in 1986.

FINEST HOUR:

Helping Saints to a fantastic second-place finish in the 1983/84 First Division.

Not many clubs in English football can claim to have produced an England goalkeeper.

Even fewer can claim to have had as many as Southampton have had. Shilton and Flowers enjoyed 13 seasons at the club between them, and earned a combined 136 caps for the Three Lions.

They combined stature with agility, ensuring Saints were never easy to score against. These were two goalkeeping all-rounders.

But which of them was better?

It's a tough call!

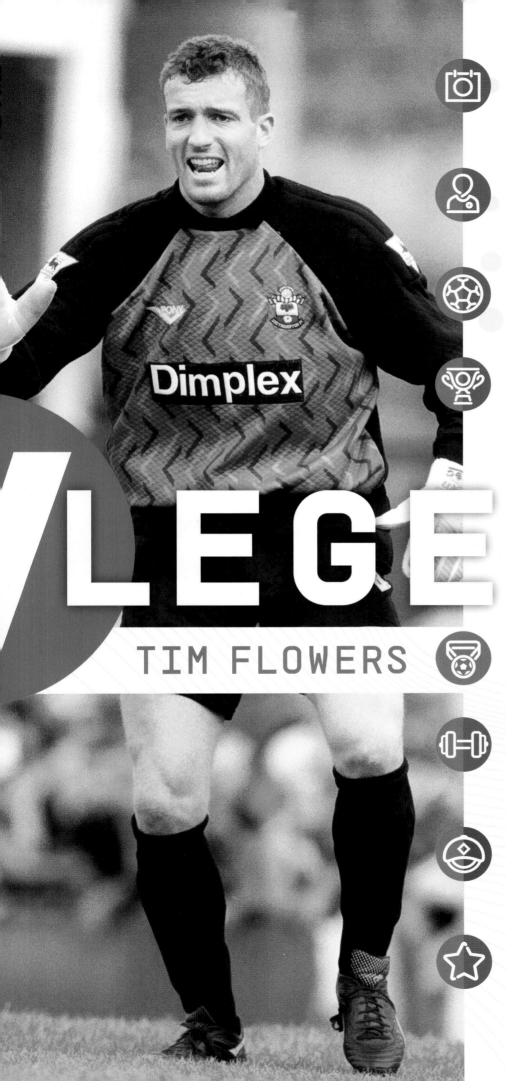

LEGEND

TIM FLOWERS

NUMBER OF SEASONS WITH THE SAINTS:
8

SOUTHAMPTON APPEARANCES:
166

SOUTHAMPTON GOALS:
0

PLAYER OF THE SEASON:
1991/92
1992/93

SOUTHAMPTON ACHIEVEMENTS:

Full Members' Cup Final runner-up (1991/92).

MAJOR STRENGTH:

A commanding presence in goal, Flowers used to dominate his area, collecting high crosses to take the pressure off his defence.

INTERNATIONAL ACTION:

Flowers earned eleven caps for the Three Lions between 1993 and 1998, and travelled as a squad member to both Euro '96 and World Cup '98.

FINEST HOUR:

After a succession of impressive seasons at Southampton, he became British football's most expensive goalkeeper when Blackburn Rovers signed him for £2.4m in 1993.

ADAM

ARMSTRONG

9

Close control in tight situations creates havoc in opposition defences - particularly when receiving the ball in the air - and nine times out of ten, when a striker receives the ball, he has his back to goal.

SOCCER SKILLS

RECEIVING THE BALL

Quite often the ball will arrive in the air, and good strikers have to be able to cope with that - controlling and turning in one movement, ready for the instant shot.

EXERCISE 1

In an area 20m x 10m, two players A and A2 test the man in the middle, B, by initially throwing the ball at him in the air, with the instruction to turn and play in to the end man - if possible using only two touches.

The middle player is changed regularly, and to make things more realistic, the end players progress to chipping the ball into the middle. The middle player is asked to receive and turn using chest, thigh, or instep.

KEY FACTORS

1 **Assess flight early - get in position.**
2 **Cushion the ball.**
3 **Be half turned as you receive.**

EXERCISE 2

A progression of this exercise is the following, where the ball is chipped or driven in to the striker from varying positions. He has to receive with his back to goal, and using just two touches in total if possible, shoot past the keeper into the goal!

To make this even more difficult, a defender can be brought in eventually. For younger children, the 'servers' should throw the ball to ensure consistent quality.

PREMIER LEAGUE 22/23

SQUAD

1 ALEX McCARTHY

GK DOB: 03/12/1989 **COUNTRY: ENGLAND**

A reliable pair of hands in Southampton's goalmouth since 2016, Alex McCarthy - the club's 2017/18 Player of the Season - has made more than 100 Saints appearances.

He will hope to reaffirm his spot in Ralph Hasenhüttl's first-team after his last campaign was unfortunately interrupted through a hamstring injury sustained during Saints' 1-1 draw at home to Brighton in December.

2 KYLE WALKER-PETERS

RB DOB: 13/04/1997 COUNTRY: ENGLAND

Last season was arguably Kyle Walker-Peters's best ever, the 25-year-old weighing in with three goals across 37 appearances in all competitions, with his form earning him a first senior England call-up in March 2022.

Having joined from Tottenham Hotspur in January 2020, Walker-Peters has gone on to establish himself as one of the Premier League's best full-backs while at Saints.

3 AINSLEY MAITLAND-NILES

CM **DOB:** 29/08/1997 **COUNTRY:** ENGLAND

With an ability to play in the heart of midfield and in both full-back positions, Southampton's loan acquisition of Ainsley Maitland-Niles on transfer deadline day looked a shrewd acquisition.

A product of the Arsenal academy, Maitland-Niles has made 132 appearances for the Gunners, winning the FA Cup with them in 2020, and has also represented England at all levels from Under-17s to the senior side, earning five full international caps, while spending time on loan at Italian giants AS Roma.

4 LYANCO

CB **DOB:** 01/02/1997 **COUNTRY:** BRAZIL

Following his signing from Torino in August 2021 on a four-year deal, Lyanco has fitted into Hasenhüttl's plans well, offering solidity on the pitch and personality off it.

The Brazilian has made a promising start to life on the south coast and particularly shone in Saints' 1-0 home win over Arsenal late last season, playing a full 90 minutes and helping keep a clean sheet.

6 DUJE **ĆALETA-CAR**

CB **DOB:** 17/09/1996 **COUNTRY:** CROATIA

Croatia international Duje Ćaleta-Car was Southampton's final signing on a busy summer transfer deadline day, further strengthening the defensive ranks as he arrived on a four-year contract.

A runner-up at the 2018 World Cup, the imposing central defender won numerous titles in Austria with Red Bull Salzburg, before then joining Marseille four years ago, twice helping the French side to finish second in the top-flight.

7 JOE **ARIBO**

CM **DOB:** 21/07/1996 **COUNTRY:** NIGERIA

Another of Southampton's new arrivals ahead of the 2022/23 season, Joe Aribo will be hoping to hit the ground running in his first campaign on the south coast.

Previously with Rangers, the Nigerian played a massive part in his former side's 2022 Europa League run, scoring in the final against Eintracht Frankfurt before their German counterparts eventually snatched victory on penalties.

8 JAMES WARD-PROWSE

CM **DOB:** 01/11/1994 **COUNTRY:** ENGLAND

Trusted with the captain's armband for the entirety of the 2021/22 season, England international and Academy graduate James Ward-Prowse continues to sparkle in Southampton's midfield.

The 27-year-old enjoyed a stunning campaign just gone, boasting an impressive seven assists and nine goals, one of which, a spectacular long-range free-kick away to Wolverhampton Wanderers in the Premier League, won Southampton's Goal of the Season award.

9 ADAM ARMSTRONG

ST **DOB:** 10/02/1997 **COUNTRY:** ENGLAND

Southampton were quick to snap-up Adam Armstrong in 2021, the striker catching the eye of many top clubs after netting 49 times in 130 appearances for former club Blackburn Rovers.

Last season, the Newcastle-born attacker showed flashes of promise, including brilliant goals at Everton and at home to Aston Villa, and will hope to see his responsibility increase this campaign.

10 **CHÉ ADAMS**

ST DOB: 13/07/1996 COUNTRY: SCOTLAND

Ché Adams's prolific goalscoring form for former club Birmingham City during the 2018/19 campaign made him one of the most sought-after youngsters in English football.

Attracted by Southampton's ability to develop young talent, the powerful forward has gone on to become one of Hasenhüttl's most trusted players, with 21 goals to his name since his arrival three years ago, eight of which came last season.

13 WILLY CABALLERO

GK **DOB:** 28/09/1981 **COUNTRY:** ARGENTINA

Entrusted with goalkeeping duties by the likes of Malaga, Manchester City and Chelsea during his career, 40-year-old Willy Caballero is undoubtedly one of the wisest goalkeeping heads in the game.

Arriving last season to cover the then-injured Alex McCarthy and Fraser Forster, the Argentine went on to make four appearances for the club, proving he still has what it takes to perform at the highest level.

15 ROMAIN PERRAUD

LB **DOB:** 22/09/1997 **COUNTRY:** FRANCE

Romain Perraud is entering his second season with the club, and has already played an important role in the left-back position since joining from Stade Brest.

The flying Frenchman enjoyed a good season last year and, despite a fractured foot in May, made 23 appearances, scoring a thunderbolt against West Ham in the FA Cup that was voted in Saints' top three goals of the season.

17 STUART ARMSTRONG
RW DOB: 30/03/1992 COUNTRY: SCOTLAND

Stuart Armstrong was one of Hasenhüttl's most influential players again last season, the creative Scotland international laying on numerous opportunities for teammates and also registering three goals in 30 appearances.

One of which, an incredible swerving finish from range against Coventry in the FA Cup, earned the 30-year-old second place in the club's annual Goal of the Season vote.

18 SÉKOU MARA
ST DOB: 30/07/2002 COUNTRY: FRANCE

Southampton beat a host of club's to the signature of French star Sékou Mara in the summer, purchasing the youngster from Bordeaux.

A France Under-21 international, Mara scored six times in 26 Ligue 1 matches for his struggling club last term. He is someone who arrives at St Mary's with huge potential and will be one to watch closely this season.

19 MOUSSA **DJENEPO**

LW DOB: **15/06/1998** COUNTRY: **MALI**

Southampton got their hands on pacey, skilful winger Moussa Djenepo from Belgian side Standard Liege in 2019. In his first two seasons on the south coast, the Mali international showed promise, scoring twice in each.

During pre-season, however, Hasenhüttl has largely used the 24-year-old as a left wing-back, which may be a position he and Romain Perraud share responsibility on.

21 TINO **LIVRAMENTO**

RB DOB: **12/11/2002** COUNTRY: ENGLAND

Another of England's most exciting young right-backs, Tino Livramento has already set the standard for his own future following an impressive first season in red and white.

Despite a serious ACL injury in April which saw the England Under-21 international's campaign cut short, Livramento still made 32 appearances, scoring his first goal in a 2-2 Premier League draw against Burnley in October 2021.

22 MOHAMMED SALISU

CB DOB: **17/04/1999** COUNTRY: **GHANA**

After excelling for Spanish side Real Valladolid in La Liga, Mohammed Salisu, then dubbed 'the wall of Valladolid' by local press, came to St Mary's in 2020.

Standing at 6' 3" the Ghanian offers a real presence at the back for Hasenhüttl's men and excels in physical one-on-one situations, helping the side to keep eight Premier League clean sheets last campaign.

23 SAM EDOZIE

LW DOB: **28/01/2003** COUNTRY: **ENGLAND**

An exciting young talent, winger Sam Edozie was one of two youngsters to join Southampton from Manchester City on transfer deadline day, and the fourth to move from the champions to St Mary's during the summer.

Edozie is an England Under-19 international and arrives at Saints with a big reputation. He moved to Manchester in July 2019 when he signed from Millwall as a scholar, and his pace and ability on the ball meant he quickly rose to further prominence in the youth ranks. Such were his performances that City manager Pep Guardiola started him in the 2021 Community Shield match against Leicester, while Edozie was also part of the first-team's pre-season this past summer.

24

MOHAMED
ELYOUNOUSSI

LW   DOB: **04/08/1994**   COUNTRY: **NORWAY**

Moroccan-born, Norwegian international Mohamed Elyounoussi, who joined the club in 2018 from Swiss team Basel, is another talented option Southampton have out wide.

Talented on the ball and with a dangerous ability to cut in from either wing, Elyounoussi was one Hasenhüttl's most regular scorers last season, netting eight times in 33 appearances across all competitions.

27 IBRAHIMA DIALLO

CM **DOB:** 08/03/1999 **COUNTRY:** FRANCE

Last season was one that Saints' young defensive midfielder Ibrahima Diallo will never forget, the Frenchman grabbing his first professional goal in a hard-fought 2-2 draw against Sheffield United in the Carabao Cup.

This season, Diallo, who joined from Stade Brest in 2020, will look to further pursue a regular place in Saints' starting line-up, having made 30 appearances last campaign.

28 JUAN LARIOS

LB **DOB:** 12/01/2004 **COUNTRY:** SPAIN

Another young arrival from Manchester City, teenage full-back Juan Larios completed a transfer from Manchester City on deadline day this summer.

He began his career in football on the books of Sevilla before moving to Barcelona in 2016 at the age of 12. Staying there for four years, the Spanish Under-19 international arrived in England in 2020, where he became a regular starter in City's Elite Development Squad in Premier League 2. Primarily a left-back, Larios is a versatile player who has also featured at right-back and on the wing, and will provide welcome competition to Ralph Hasenhüttl's first-team squad.

31 GAVIN **BAZUNU**

GK DOB: 20/02/2002 COUNTRY: REPUBLIC OF IRELAND

Arriving on the south coast following three years with Pep Guardiola's Manchester City, young 20-year-old goalkeeper Gavin Bazunu has already made his name on the international stage, solidifying his place as the Republic of Ireland's first choice, with ten caps.

He hit the ground running during Saints' pre-season tour of Austria, showcasing his ability with a magnificent one-handed save from RB Leipzig's Dominic Szoboszlai.

32 THEO **WALCOTT**

RW **DOB:** 16/03/1989 **COUNTRY:** ENGLAND

Enjoying his second spell on the south coast having made his Premier League debut with Southampton more than 15 years ago, Theo Walcott has added wisdom to his ever-growing arsenal of traits.

The 33-year-old didn't manage to add to the 78 Premier League goals he already has to his name last season, but did make 12 appearances in all competitions.

37 ARMEL **BELLA-KOTCHAP**

CB **DOB:** 11/12/2001 **COUNTRY:** GERMANY

Another new recruit, 20-year-old Armel Bella-Kotchap only needed 19 Bundesliga starts with former club VfL Bochum to prove his ability and secure a move to the Premier League.

The centre-back boasts traits that fit well with Hasenhüttl's style, his considerable pace, strength and physicality adding an extra layer of protection to Southampton's high defensive line.

PREMIER LEAGUE 22/23 SQUAD

45 ROMÉO LAVIA

CM **DOB:** 06/01/2004 **COUNTRY:** BELGIUM

Crowned Player of the Season in 2020 for Manchester City's Elite Development squad before securing his move to St Mary's, Roméo Lavia's substantial potential is unquestionable.

Just 18-years-old, the Belgium Under-19 international was included six times in City's squad last season, including both legs of their Champions League semi-final against Real Madrid. He will likely be part of Hasenhüttl's first-team plans on a regular basis.

SOUTHAMPTON FC

TRUE OR FALSE

Here are ten fun footy True or False teasers for you to tackle!

GOOD LUCK...

ANSWERS ON PAGE 62

2. The FIFA World Cup in 2026 is due to be hosted in the USA, Mexico and Canada

3. Manchester City's former ground was called Maine Park

1. England star Harry Kane has only ever played club football for Tottenham Hotspur

4. Liverpool's Jurgen Klopp has never managed the German national team

5. Gareth Southgate succeeded Roy Hodgson as England manager

6. Manchester United's Old Trafford has the largest capacity in the Premier League

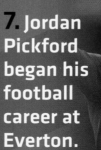

7. Jordan Pickford began his football career at Everton.

8. Huddersfield Town's nickname is the Terriers

9. Nathan Redmond joined the Saints from Norwich City in 2017

10. Ché Adams scored seven Premier League goals for Southampton in 2021/22

MOHAMMED
SALISU
22

SOUTHAMPTON FC

Sammy Saint is hiding in the crowd in five different places as the Southampton fans celebrate.

Can you find all five?

ANSWERS ON PAGE 62

FAN'TASTIC

MOUSSA
DJENEPO
19

Defending is not just about stopping the attackers and clearing your lines. Making the best of possession you have just won is vital - although the danger has to be cleared, it is important for your team to keep hold of the ball.

SOCCER SKILLS

LONG PASSES

When passing your way out of defence, and short, side-foot passes are not possible, the longer pass, driven over the heads of midfield players, can be used.

EXERCISE

In an area 40m x 10m, A1 and A2 try to pass accurately to each other, with a defender B, in the middle between them. Player B must attempt to stop the pass if possible, and A1 and A2, must keep the ball within the area of the grids.

After each successful long pass, the end player will exchange a shorter pass with B before passing long again, thus keeping the exercise realistic and also keeping the defender in the middle involved. The player in the middle should be changed every few minutes, and a 'count' of successful passes made for each player.

KEY FACTORS

1 Approach at an angle.
2 Non-kicking foot placed next to the ball.
3 Eye on the ball.
4 Strike underneath the ball & follow through.

Practice is the key to striking a consistently accurate long pass and to developing the timing and power required.

The same end result could be achieved by bending the pass around the defender instead of over him, and this pass could be practised in the same exercise, by striking the football on its outer edge (instead of underneath) which will impart the spin required to make the ball 'bend' around the defender - not an easy skill!

10m

40m

TRAIN TO WIN

Making sure that you are fit, healthy and fully prepared is key to success in whatever challenge you are taking on. Those three factors are certainly vital for professional footballers and also for any young aspiring player who plays for his or her school or local football team. The importance of fitness, health and preparation are key factors behind the work that goes into preparing the Southampton players to perform at their maximum on matchday.

The Saints players will need to demonstrate peak levels of fitness if they want to feature in Ralph Hasenhüttl's team. Before anyone can think of pulling on a red and white shirt and stepping out at St Mary's, they will have had to perform well in training to have shown the manager, his coaches and fitness staff that they are fully fit and ready for the physical challenges that await them on a matchday.

Regardless of whether training takes place at the training ground or at the stadium, the players' fitness remains an all-important factor. Of course time spent practicing training drills and playing small-sided games will help a player's fitness, but there is lots of work undertaken just to ensure maximum levels of fitness are reached.

Away from the training pitches the players will spend a great deal of time in the gymnasium partaking in their own personal work-outs. Bikes, treadmills and weights will all form part of helping the players reach and maintain a top level of fitness.

Over the course of a week the players will take part in many warm-up and aerobic sessions and even complete yoga and Pilates classes to help with core strength and general fitness. The strength and conditioning coaches at the club work tirelessly to do all they can to make sure that the players you see in action are at their physical peak come kick-off.

While the manager and his staff will select the team and agree the tactics, analysts will provide the players and staff with details on the opposition's strengths, weaknesses and their likely approach to the match.

Suffice to say the training ground is a busy place and no stone is left unturned in preparation for the big match!

PLAYER
OF THE
SEASON

JAMES
WARD-PROWSE

DOMINIC
BALLARD

Following a highly impressive 2021/22 season in which Southampton's skipper netted on nine occasions in 38 league appearances, James Ward-Prowse scooped a deserved hat-trick of accolades at Saints' annual end of season awards ceremony in May, the coveted Fans' Player of the Season title arguably the pick of the bunch.

Widely respected for his ability to set the tempo and create offensive opportunities from midfield, the 27-year-old, in addition to his hefty goal contribution, also registered seven Premier League assists last season, capping his most productive campaign in red and white.

The Englishman's sustained development under Ralph Hasenhüttl's guidance in recent years has been clear for all to see and he has now blossomed into the Austrian's trusted captain. Ward-Prowse also holds an incredible record for on-pitch minutes, as the first midfielder to play every minute of consecutive Premier League campaigns, completing a full 90 for 77 matches in a row.

However, perhaps his greatest footballing asset is his remarkable ability from dead-ball situations. Ward-Prowse directly found the net four times from free-kicks last season, increasing his all-time tally to 14, behind only the legendary David Beckham (18).

With that in mind, it's unsurprising that Ward-Prowse has found himself in England manager Gareth Southgate's plans more regularly, the number eight earning three more caps last season, scoring in a 5-0 World Cup qualifying win away to Andorra, before featuring in a 3-0 win over Ivory Coast and a 0-0 draw against current European champions Italy.

Ahead of the new 2022/23 season, Ward-Prowse is keen to use the success of last season as a platform to reach even higher goals: "To receive that recognition was pretty special and I'm using it to hopefully take me to the next level.

SCHOLAR
OF THE YEAR

Winner of Southampton's prestigious Scholar of the Year award for the 2021/22 season was Dominic Ballard.

The 17-year-old striker enjoyed a fruitful last season across Saints' Under-18 and B teams, netting 26 times in 41 appearances, which included impressive back-to-back hat-tricks in the Under-18 Premier League away to Aston Villa and West Brom.

In April, Ballard's fine contribution was rewarded by the club through the offer of a full-time professional contract, the first of his career. The deal came nearly a decade after he initially arrived on the south coast in 2013, something the youngster branded "a dream come true".

"It's something that I've only ever dreamed of," he said. "Now that it's happening it's a dream come true.

"It was an easy decision because of how good the club is and how it feels to be here. I'm really enjoying it and it's a credit to the way we play here, it suits my attributes so well."

DREAM TEAM

Pick your ultimate Southampton dream team and design them a kit!

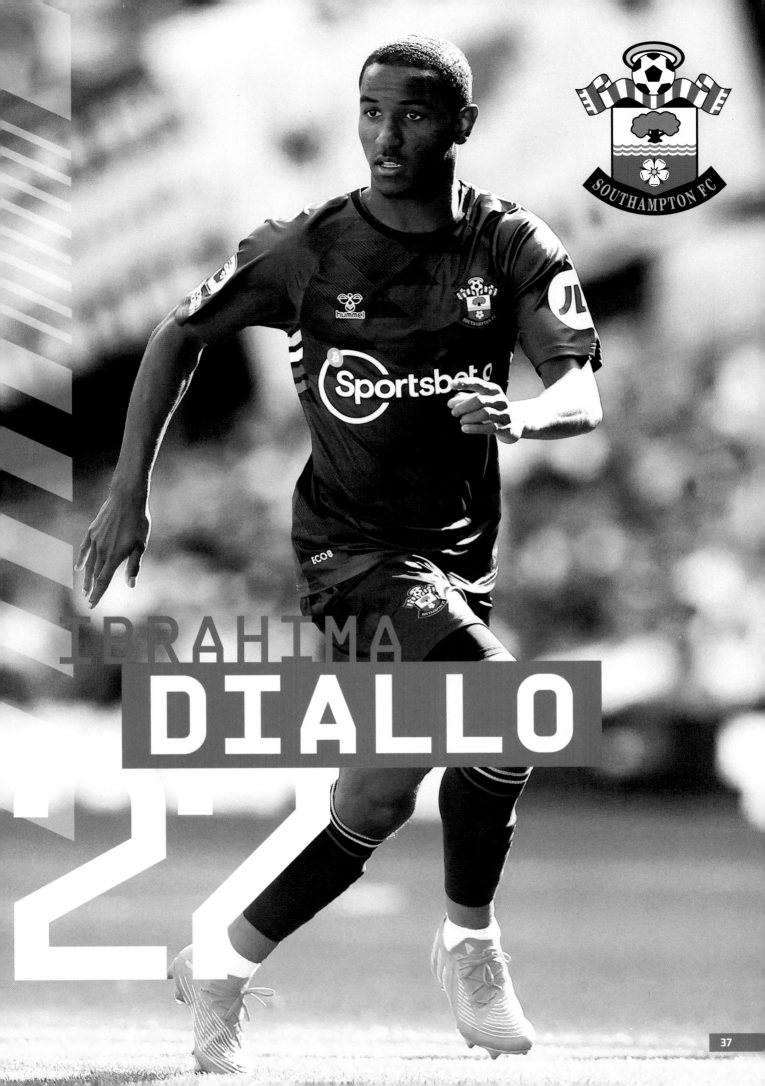

IBRAHIMA
DIALLO

27

SOUTHAMPTON FC

SOUTHAMPTON FC

PREMIER LEAGUE
DANGER MEN

20 TOP-FLIGHT STARS TO WATCH OUT FOR DURING 2022/23...

ARSENAL
GABRIEL JESUS

The Gunners completed the signing of Brazilian international striker Gabriel Jesus from Premier League champions Manchester City in July 2022.

A real penalty box predator, Jesus netted 95 goals in 236 appearances in a trophy-laden spell for City and Arsenal will be hopeful he can continue his impressive goals-to-games ratio at the Emirates Stadium.

ASTON VILLA
EMI BUENDIA

Now in his second season at Villa Park, following a big money move from Norwich City, a great deal will be expected of Argentinean international midfielder Emi Buendia in 2022/23.

A highly skilful and creative player, Buendia has the ability to create chances for teammates and score vital goals himself.

BOURNEMOUTH
KIEFFER MOORE

Giant front man Kieffer Moore chipped in with four goals in three games to help Bournemouth secure promotion to the Premier League last season.

The former Cardiff City man will be keen to prove his worth at Premier League level in 2022/23 in order to cement his place in Wales' squad for the 2022 FIFA World Cup finals in Qatar.

BRENTFORD
KEANE LEWIS-POTTER

England under-21 star Keane Lewis-Potter enjoyed an exceptional Championship campaign with Hull City in 2021/22 and that prompted Brentford to spend a club record fee to bring the exciting 21-year-old to West London.

A true attacker who can operate off of either flank, Lewis-Potter will be relishing the challenge of showcasing his skills at Premier League level.

BRIGHTON & HA
LEANDRO TROSSARD

After weighing in with eight Premier League goals last season, Belgian international winger Trossard has widely become recognised as the Seagulls' main creative force.

Hugging the left touchline and cutting inside to play in a teammate or striking for goal himself, Trossard is another player who will be looking to feature in the forthcoming World Cup.

CRYSTAL PALACE
WILFRIED ZAHA

Players may come and go at Selhurst Park, but the constant threat offered by the Crystal Palace club legend Wilfried Zaha remains firmly in place.

An exciting forward who loves to take opponents on in one-on-one situations, Zaha has now amassed over 400 appearances for the club across his two spells at Selhurst Park, and will be looking to fly the Eagles into the top half of the Premier League table.

CHELSEA
MASON MOUNT

Having progressed through the academy system at Stamford Bridge, attacking midfielder Mason Mount has become one of the first names on both the Chelsea and England teamsheet.

Mount hit eleven Premier League goals last season and boss Graham Potter will be keen to see more of the same as Chelsea look to put pressure on Liverpool and Manchester City in 2022/23.

EVERTON
JORDAN PICKFORD

Firmly established as first choice keeper for club and country, Jordan has been a reliable last line of defence for the Toffees since joining the club in summer 2017.

A host of match-saving games last season were rewarded with the Player of the Season award and the England No.1 has now played over 200 games for Everton.

FULHAM
ALEKSANDAR MITROVIC

Having fired home a record-breaking 43 Championship goals for Fulham in their title-winning campaign last season, all eyes will be on Aleksandar Mitrovic in 2022/23.

If Fulham are to shake off their yo-yo club tag, then the top-flight goalscoring form of their powerful Serbian striker is going to be key.

LIVERPOOL
MOHAMED SALAH

Together with goalkeeper Alisson and inspirational defender Virgil van Dijk, Liverpool forward Mo Salah has been the catalyst for the Reds' success in recent seasons.

The Egyptian superstar jointly topped the Premier League scoring charts with Spurs' Son Heung-min last season as Liverpool enjoyed a domestic cup double.

LEEDS UNITED
PATRICK BAMFORD

After suffering an injury-hit 2021/22, Leeds United striker Patrick Bamford will be hopeful that 2022/23 offers him the chance to demonstrate the form that won him a first full England cap in September 2021.

A versatile front man who can play as a lone striker or in a pair, Bamford can also operate as an attacking midfielder from either flank.

LEICESTER CITY
JAMIE VARDY

The goalscoring hero of Leicester City's sensational 2014/15 Premier League title triumph, striker Jamie Vardy once again topped the Foxes' scoring charts last season.

An energetic forward, full of running, Jamie never gives defenders a moment of peace, and will once again be the one to watch for goals at King Power Stadium in 2022/23.

MANCHESTER CITY
ERLING HAALAND

Manchester City pulled off the biggest summer transfer coup when they lured Norwegian striker Erling Haaland from Borussia Dortmund to the Etihad Stadium for 2022/23.

Boasting a phenomenal strike rate at Dortmund and with his national team too, Haaland is sure to bring goals galore to the Premier League champions.

MANCHESTER UNITED
BRUNO FERNANDES

Attacking midfielder Bruno has become the heartbeat of the Red Devils' forward play since signing from Sporting Lisbon.

Blessed with a wide range of passing skills, the 28-year-old Portuguese international has the knack of unlocking even the tightest of defences.

TOTTENHAM HOTSPUR
SON HEUNG-MIN

South Korean superstar Son ended the 2021/22 season by picking up the Premier League Golden Boot as joint top goalscorer along with Liverpool's Mohamed Salah.

Forming an almost telepathic partnership with England captain Harry Kane, Tottenham Hotspur will certainly be a team to watch if Son repeats his lethal form in front of goal again in 2022/23.

NEWCASTLE UNITED
BRUNO GUIMARAES

After joining the Magpies from Lyon in January 2022, Brazilian midfielder Bruno has become a real cult hero with the fans at St James' Park.

Bruno scored five Premier League goals in 17 games last season and looks set to be one of the first names on Eddie Howe's teamsheet in 22/23.

WEST HAM UNITED
JARROD BOWEN

Blessed with the ability to operate in a variety of attacking positions, Jarrod Bowen enjoyed an exceptional 2021/22 campaign.

The 25-year-old netted 18 goals in all competitions and made 51 appearances as the Hammers enjoyed a top-half finish and reached the semi-finals of the Europa League. He was also handed an England debut in June 2022.

NOTTINGHAM FOREST
DEAN HENDERSON

Forest made a real statement of intent following their promotion to the Premier League when they completed the season-long loan signing of the Man United keeper.

Capped by England, Dean will hope his City Ground performances can push him into England boss Gareth Southgate's thoughts for the 2022 FIFA World Cup finals in Qatar.

SOUTHAMPTON
JAMES WARD-PROWSE

One of the very best dead ball deliverers, Saints skipper Ward-Prowse has progressed through the academy ranks at St Mary's to play over 350 first-team games for the club.

James is another England star who will hope to be on the plane for Qatar 2022.

WOLVES
GONCALO GUEDES

Wanderers boosted their attacking options when they completed the signing of Portugal forward Goncalo Guedes from Valencia at the start of the 2022/23 season.

Capped on over 30 occasions by Portugal, the 25-year-old is well known to Wolves' boss Bruno Lage having played for him at Benfica earlier in his career.

MULTIPLE CHOICE

Here are ten Multiple Choice questions to challenge your footy knowledge!

GOOD LUCK...

ANSWERS ON PAGE 62

1. What was the name of Tottenham Hotspur's former ground?

A) White Rose Park
B) White Foot Way
C) White Hart Lane

2. Which club did Steven Gerrard leave to become Aston Villa manager?

A) Liverpool,
B) Glasgow Rangers
C) LA Galaxy

3. Mohamed Salah and Son Heung-min were joint winners of the Premier League Golden Boot as the division's top scorers in 2021/22.

How many goals did they score?

A) 23 B) 24   C) 25

4. What is the nationality of Manchester United boss Erik ten Hag?

A) Swiss   B) Dutch
C) Swedish

5. Where do Everton play their home games?

A) Goodison Road
B) Goodison Way
C) Goodison Park

6. From which club did Arsenal sign goalkeeper Aaron Ramsdale?

A) Sheffield United
B) Stoke City
C) AFC Bournemouth

7. What is Raheem Sterling's middle name?

A) Shaun
B) Shaquille
C) Silver

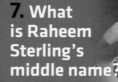

Against which country did James Ward-Prowse make his senior England debut?

A) Lithuania
B) France
C) Germany

8. Who won the 2021/22 League One Play-Off final?

A) Wigan Athletic
B) Sunderland
C) Rotherham United

9. How many times have the Saints won the FA Cup?

A) Once, B) Twice
C) Three times

42

JAMES

WARD-PROWSE

8

NUMBER OF SEASONS WITH THE SAINTS:

2.5

SOUTHAMPTON APPEARANCES:

80

SOUTHAMPTON GOALS:

7

PLAYER OF THE SEASON:

2015/16

LEGEND

VIRGIL VAN DIJK

SOUTHAMPTON ACHIEVEMENTS:

EFL Cup runners-up (2016/17).

MAJOR STRENGTH:

Marauding runs out of defence.

INTERNATIONAL ACTION:

Van Dijk made his Netherlands debut in 2015 and it took him fewer than three years to become Dutch captain. Approaching 50 caps, he is yet to compete in a major tournament, but is looking forward to World Cup 2022.

FINEST HOUR:

Replacing José Fonte as Saints' captain in January 2017

For Southampton fans, seeing Virgil van Dijk shining performances for Liverpool each week must be a bittersweet feeling. They helped to make the Dutch captain the domineering centre-back he is today, but they no longer have him on their books.

Francis Benali was not similar to Van Dijk in that way, he was a full-back after all. But he is rightly considered one of the biggest legends in the history of the club. Benali was a real servant to Saints, and his association with the club lasted 19 years.

Both modern Southampton greats, but which comes out on top?

NUMBER OF SEASONS WITH THE SAINTS:

15

SOUTHAMPTON APPEARANCES:

359

SOUTHAMPTON GOALS:

1

PLAYER OF THE SEASON:

Amazingly, despite all of his attributes, Francis Benali was never a winner of the Player of the Season award.

LEGEND

FRANCIS BENALI

SOUTHAMPTON ACHIEVEMENTS:

Full Members' Cup Final runner-up (1991/92), FA Cup runner-up (2002/03),

MAJOR STRENGTH:

Defensive astuteness from full-back

INTERNATIONAL ACTION:

To the dismay of the Saints fans, Benali has never represented England at international level despite his solid defensive performances for his club.

FINEST HOUR:

Scoring his only Southampton goal, against Leicester City, in a 1997 Premier League match. The goal was assisted by fellow Saints legend Matt Le Tissier.

CLUB SEARCH

```
M A S D D E T I N U R E T S E H C N A M
K P W H M F Y A G I S G F Z E N O P H S
S M A N C H E S T E R C I T Y J B F O E
W N A E L T G I R C I A S B D R I U J T
K E F R U P S T O H M A H N E T T O T G
H Q S B D D B L B S V U S N D H O R S B
C A F T X E H O R Y S N T H A K J M E E
A G Y J H W T U O Q C F N M C A L V R C
U O U T S A R I L P O D P K L P E A O A
H T S U I G M A N R A T P L U R T D F L
T P T H P C N U D U O M I S T A F E M A
U I T W V E R A N N E V F O W E P G A P
O R M E S J W E P I N L N L E S U L H L
M O K R O S U V T O T A T M N L C I G A
E M A H L U F G T S K E K S D E B M N T
N N L D Q F C S N P E W D H A H O A I S
R S I A J B A O A S Y C B O O C N X T Y
U H D R Z L O O P R E V I L U L W J T R
O T E C D E T I N U S D E E L R A E O C
B R I G H T O N & H O V E A L B I O N T
```

Arsenal
Aston Villa
Bournemouth
Brentford
Brighton & Hove Albion

Chelsea
Crystal Palace
Everton
Fulham
Leeds United

Leicester City
Liverpool
Manchester City
Manchester United
Newcastle United

Nottingham Forest
Southampton
Tottenham Hotspur
West Ham United
Wolverhampton Wanderers

ANSWERS ON PAGE 62

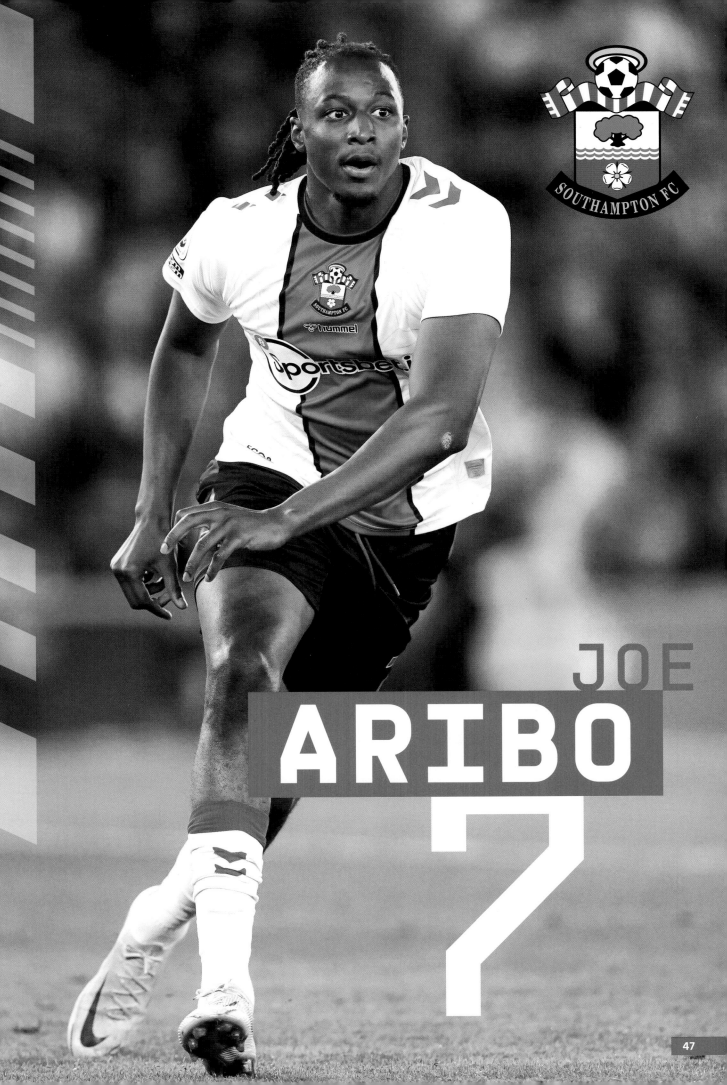

JOE
ARIBO
7

NAME THE SEASON

Can you recall the campaign when these magic moments occurred?

ANSWERS ON PAGE 62

GOOD LUCK...

1. In which season did Chelsea last win the UEFA Champions League?

2. When were Manchester United last Premier League champions?

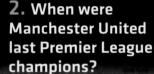

3. At the end of which season were England crowned World Cup winners?

4. In which season did Aleksandar Mitrovic net 43 Championship goals for Fulham?

5. In which season did Leicester City become Premier League champions?

6. When did Tottenham Hotspur last reach the League Cup final?

7. In which season were Sheffield United last promoted to the Premier League?

8. When did Manchester City win their first Premier League title?

9. During which season did the Saints record an 8-0 Premier League victory over Sunderland?

10. In which season did Southampton begin playing at St Mary's Stadium?

48

WHICH BALL?

Can you work out which is the actual match ball in these two action pics?

SOUTHAMPTON FC

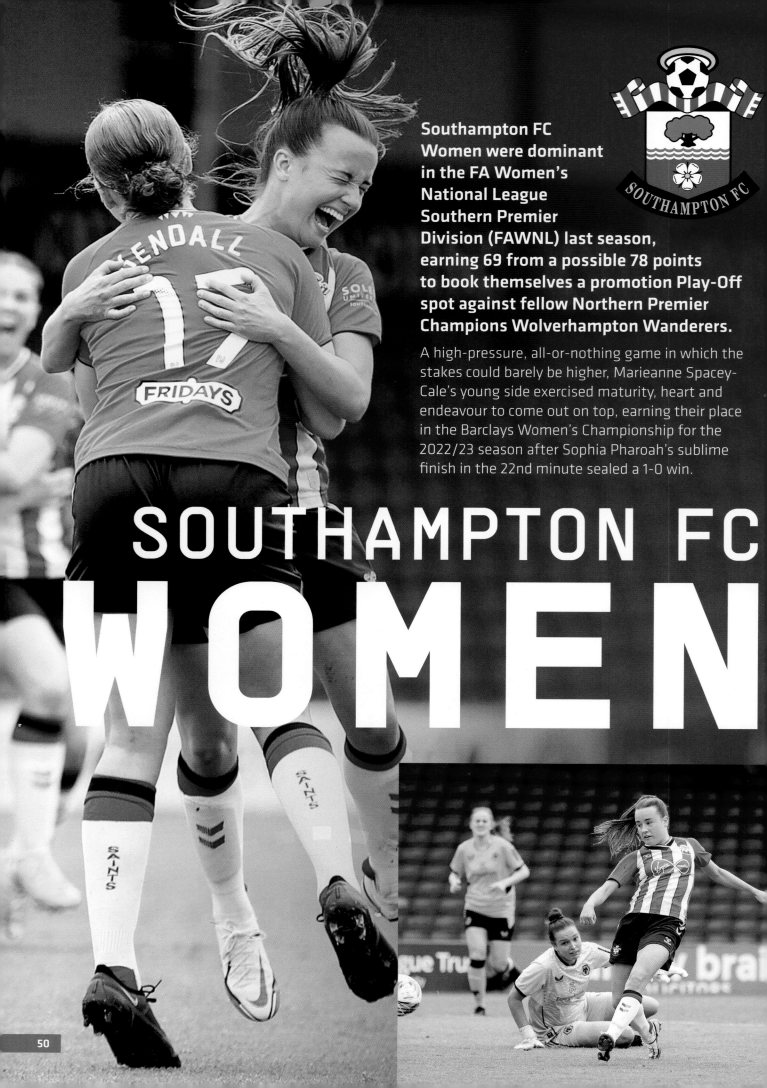

Southampton FC Women were dominant in the FA Women's National League Southern Premier Division (FAWNL) last season, earning 69 from a possible 78 points to book themselves a promotion Play-Off spot against fellow Northern Premier Champions Wolverhampton Wanderers.

A high-pressure, all-or-nothing game in which the stakes could barely be higher, Marieanne Spacey-Cale's young side exercised maturity, heart and endeavour to come out on top, earning their place in the Barclays Women's Championship for the 2022/23 season after Sophia Pharoah's sublime finish in the 22nd minute sealed a 1-0 win.

SOUTHAMPTON FC
WOMEN

Despite their recent success, it hasn't always been plain sailing for the women's team. During both of their 2019/20 and 2020/21 seasons, Saints found themselves in pole position for promotion into the FAWNL Southern Premier before nationwide league curtailments were announced by the FA due to the COVID-19 pandemic, delaying the squad's progression. They were, however, promoted after that second campaign, as The FA invited applications for upward movement from deserving clubs.

Ahead of their first-ever season in the Championship, the decision has been made for the women's programme to adopt a full-time model, ensuring the squad benefits from multi-disciplinary support at Staplewood Campus, including access to all facilities and expertise.

In order to be best prepared for the task at hand, Spacey-Cale has also been busy in the transfer market, bringing in a mix of experience and youth through the signings of goalkeeper Sophie Harris, defender Paige Peake, midfielder Megan Wynne and forwards Beth Lumsden, Lexi Lloyd-Smith and Katie Wilkinson.

"It's exciting to have them on board and to have them as part of our squad" said Spacey-Cale. "They've settled in really well and each of them brings a freshness to our squad. Everyone is enthusiastic and eager to get going and that's already showing in training."

SOUTHAMPTON FC

1. WHO AM I?

2. WHO AM I?

3. WHO AM I?

4. WHO AM I?

SOUTHAMPTON FC

WHO ARE YER?

Can you figure out who each of these Saints stars is?

SOUTHAMPTON FC

5. WHO AM I?

7. WHO AM I?

8. WHO AM I?

6. WHO AM I?

ANSWERS ON PAGE 62

KYLE
WALKER-PETERS

2

TRUE
COLOURS

Colour in
this picture
of Kyle
Walker-Peters

TOP 10

MY TOP 10...

MOMENTS OF THIS YEAR

1.
2.
3.
4.
5.
6.
7.
8.
9.
10.

MY TOP 10...

SAINTS STARS OF ALL TIME

1.
2.
3.
4.
5.
6.
7.
8.
9.
10.

MY TOP 10...

SOUTHAMPTON MEMORIES

1.
2.
3.
4.
5.
6.
7.
8.
9.
10.

MY TOP 10...

RESOLUTIONS FOR 2023

1.
2.
3.
4.
5.
6.
7.
8.
9.
10.

COVER THE WALL
IN POSTERS!

ST MARY'S
STADIUM
SO14

SOUTHAMPTON FC

NUMBER OF SEASONS WITH THE SAINTS:

16

SOUTHAMPTON APPEARANCES:

540

SOUTHAMPTON GOALS:

209

PLAYER OF THE SEASON:

**1989/90
93/94 & 94/95**

LEGEND

LE TISSIER

SOUTHAMPTON ACHIEVEMENTS:

Full Members' Cup runner-up (1991/92).

MAJOR STRENGTH:

Ridiculous technique and ability, dribbling from deep and intricately entering the box to score.

INTERNATIONAL ACTION:

Many people argue Le Tissier should have played more times for England. The Guernsey-born striker represented the Three Lions eight times between 1994 and 1997, never finding the back of the net.

FINEST HOUR:

His stupendous flick-and-volley free-kick against Wimbledon in 1994.

The Saints can claim to have had some real stars play for them over their long and storied history, but these two perhaps, scream Southampton more than any others.

Two undoubted legends of the club, Matt Le Tissier and James Ward-Prowse have shown their loyalty to Southampton by remaining on the South Coast even when other clubs tried to prise them away. True one-club men.

Yet again, it's a very tough call...

LEGEND

WARD-PROWSE

NUMBER OF SEASONS WITH THE SAINTS:

12 & COUNTING...

SOUTHAMPTON APPEARANCES:

365

SOUTHAMPTON GOALS:

45

PLAYER OF THE SEASON:

2020/21
2021/22

SOUTHAMPTON ACHIEVEMENTS:

EFL Cup runner-up (2016/17).

MAJOR STRENGTH:

Manchester City manager Pep Guardiola believes he is the best free-kick taker in the world.

INTERNATIONAL ACTION:

Heavily capped for England at youth level, Ward-Prowse is a member of Gareth Southgate's current England team - and has two goals from his eleven caps.

FINEST HOUR:

Scoring two outrageous free-kicks in the same game, as Saints won 4–3 at Aston Villa in a November 2020 Premier League clash.

IDENTIFY THE STAR

SOUTHAMPTON FC

Can you put a name to the football stars in these ten teasers?

GOOD LUCK...

ANSWERS ON PAGE 62

1. Manchester City's title-winning 'keeper Ederson shared the 2021/22 Golden Glove award for the number of clean sheets with which Premier League rival?

2. Which Portuguese superstar re-joined Manchester United in the 2021/22 season?

3. Can you name the Brazilian forward who joined Aston Villa in May 2022 following a loan spell at Villa Park?

4. Who became Arsenal manager in 2019?

5. Who scored the winning goal in the 2021/22 UEFA Champions League final?

6. After 550 games for West Ham United, which long-serving midfielder announced his retirement in 2022?

7. Who took the mantle of scoring Brentford's first Premier League goal?

8. Who scored the final goal for Manchester City in their 2021/22 Premier League title-winning season?

9. Before 22/23 who was the last Saints player to score a Premier League hat-trick?

10. Can you name the Nigerian midfielder who joined the Saints from Rangers ahead of the 2022/23 season?

SOUTHAMPTON FC

STUART
ARMSTRONG
17

ANSWERS

PAGE 26 · TRUE OR FALSE

1. False (Harry played on loan for Leyton Orient, Millwall, Norwich City & Leicester City). **2.** True.
3. False (it was called Maine Road). **4.** True.
5. False (Gareth succeeded Sam Allardyce). **6.** True.
7. False (Jordan began his career at Sunderland).
8. True. **9.** False (he joined in 2016). **10.** True.

PAGE 28 · CLASSIC FAN'TASTIC

PAGE 42 · MULTIPLE CHOICE

1. C.   **2.** B.   **3.** A.   **4.** B.   **5.** C.
6. A.   **7.** B.   **8.** B.   **9.** A.   **10.** C.

PAGE 46 · CLUB SEARCH

Wolverhampton Wanderers.

PAGE 48 · NAME THE SEASON

1. 2020/21.   **2.** 2012/13.   **3.** 1965/66.
4. 2021/22.   **5.** 2015/16.   **6.** 2020/21.
7. 2018/19.   **8.** 2011/12.   **9.** 2014/15.
10. 2001/02.

PAGE 49 · WHICH BALL?

Top. Ball G.   **Bottom.** Ball D.

PAGE 52 · WHO ARE YER?

1. Sekou Mara. **2.** Joe Aribo. **3.** Mohamed Elyounoussi.
4. Sekou Mara. **5.** Adam Armstrong. **6.** Armel Bella-Kotchap.
7. Romain Perraud. **8.** Ché Adams.

PAGE 60 · IDENTIFY THE STAR

1. Allison Becker (Liverpool). **2.** Cristiano Ronaldo.
3. Philippe Coutinho. **4.** Mikel Arteta.
5. Vinicius Junior. **6.** Mark Noble. **7.** Sergi Canos.
8. Ilkay Gundogan. **9.** Sadio Mane (v Manchester City 2014/15). **10.** Joe Aribo.